Believe in the magic

"The only way to achieve the impossible is to believe it is possible."

"Success is not final,
failure is not fatal: It
is the courage to
continue that counts.

"Believe you can and you're halfway there."

"The future belongs
to those who believe
in the beauty of
their dreams

✦

"Your limitation—
it's only your
imagination."

"Push yourself,
because no one else is
going to do it for you."

""The greatest happiness of life is the conviction that we are loved; loved for ourselves, or rather, loved in spite of ourselves."

"In love there are two things- bodies and words."

"There is always madness in love. But there is also always some reason in madness."

"Courage is the most important of all the virtues because without courage, you can't practice any other virtue consistently."

"The most courageous act is still to think for yourself. Aloud."

"If your dreams don't scare you, they are too small."

"What we fear of
doing most is
usually what we most
need to do."

"Every
accomplishment
starts with the
decision to try."

"People who wonder if the glass is half empty or half full miss the point. The glass is refillable."

"People often say that motivation doesn't last. Well, neither does bathing; that's why we recommend it daily."

"If you think you are too small to make a difference, try sleeping with a mosquito."

"The best revenge
is massive
success."

"Be humble. Be hungry. And always be the hardest worker in the room."

"There are no secrets to success. It is the result of preparation, hard work, and learning from failure."

"A river cuts through a rock not because of its power but its persistence."

"Sometimes later
becomes never.
Do it now."

"Nothing will
work unless you
do."

"The most difficult thing is the decision to act, the rest is merely tenacity."

"You cannot swim for new horizons until you have courage to lose sight of the shore."

"To handle yourself use your head; to handle others, use your heart."

""Learn from the mistakes of others. You can't live long enough to make them all yourselves."

"If you are not growing, you are dying."

"Learn a language, and you'll avoid a war."

"Life shrinks or
expands in proportion
to one's courage."

"The biggest adventure you can ever take is to live the life of your dreams."

"Life is like a coin.
You can spend it any
way you wish, but you
only spend it once."

"Mistakes are a fact of life. It is the response to the error that counts."

"If everything was perfect, you would never learn and you would never grow."

"If we don't change,
we don't grow. If we
don't grow, we aren't
really living."

"Life doesn't have to be perfect to be wonderful."

"The most important trip you may take in life is meeting people halfway."

"Challenges are what make life interesting and overcoming them is what makes life meaningful."

"Life isn't about finding yourself. Life is about creating yourself."

"Life is like riding
a bicycle. To keep
your balance, you
must keep moving."

"Start each day with a positive thought and a grateful heart."

"The most wasted of all days is one without laughter."

"In order to write
about life first
you must live it."

"You only live once,
but if you do it right,
once is enough."

"It always seems impossible until it is done."

"Failure will never
overtake me if my
determination to
succeed is strong
enough."

"Success is walking from failure to failure with no loss of enthusiasm."

"The only limit to our realization of tomorrow will be our doubts of today."

"The only way to do great work is to love what you do."

"Believe in yourself.
You are braver than
you think, more
talented than you know,
and capable of more
than you imagine."

"Success is not the key to happiness. Happiness is the key to success. If you love what you are doing, you will be successful."

"You are never too old to set another goal or to dream a new dream."

"Failure will never overtake me if my determination to succeed is strong enough."

"Don't watch the clock;
do what it does. Keep
going."

"Success is walking from failure to failure with no loss of enthusiasm."

"The only limit to our realization of tomorrow will be our doubts of today."

"The only way to do great work is to love what you do."

"Believe in yourself. You are braver than you think, more talented than you know, and capable of more than you imagine."

"Success is not the key to happiness. Happiness is the key to success. If you love what you are doing, you will be successful."

"You are never too old
to set another goal or to
dream a new dream."

"Failure will never overtake me if my determination to succeed is strong enough."

"Your life does not get better by chance, it gets better by change."

"Success is not just about making money. It's about making a difference."

"The only way to achieve the impossible is to believe it is possible."

"Success is not final, failure is not fatal: It is the courage to continue that counts."

"Believe you can
and you're
halfway there."

"The future belongs to those who believe in the beauty of their dreams."ve in the

magic

"Success is walking from failure to failure with no loss of enthusiasm."

"Be fearless in the pursuit of what sets your soul on fire."

"The difference between a stumbling block and a stepping stone is how you use them."

LOVE YOURSELF !!!!!

www.ingramcontent.com/pod-product-compliance
Lightning Source LLC
Chambersburg PA
CBHW040300240726
48664CB00006B/1312